A DAY-BOOK OF PRAYER

FOR THE PRIVATE USE OF YOUNG MEN AND WOMEN

SEVENTH EDITION

Published for
THE CHURCH OF SCOTLAND
COMMITTEE ON YOUTH
by
COMMITTEE ON PUBLICATIONS
121 GEORGE STREET, EDINBURGH
232 ST VINCENT STREET, GLASGOW

Printed in Great Britain
by Turnbull & Spears, Edinburgh

CONTENTS

NOTE

This book, while consisting mainly of new material, contains a number of short prayers borrowed from ancient or modern sources. These are marked by an asterisk in the text, and a list is here appended which, used with reference to the asterisks, will enable any one to discover the sources. It has not been thought necessary so to mark the verses of hymns that are used. These are nearly all from hymns included in the Revised Edition of the Church Hymnary; and wherever numbers of hymns are given for reference, it is to that Hymnary that they refer.

Grateful acknowledgment is made to the following owners of copyright for permission to include copyright material:—Messrs Hodder & Stoughton, Ltd. (for passages from Moffatt's *The New Testament: A New Translation*); Messrs James Clarke & Co., Ltd. (for the lines from a hymn by M. Farningham on p. 49); Messrs James Nisbet & Co., Ltd. (for the lines from a hymn by F. R. Havergal on p. 63); Messrs Macmillan & Co., Ltd. (for the lines from hymns by Charles Kingsley and J. C. Shairp on pp. 25 and 17 respectively, and for the prayer by B. F. Westcott on p. 19); the Society for Promoting Christian Knowledge (for the Prayers by Christina G. Rossetti on pp. 15, 59, and 63); the Student Christian Movement (for prayers on pp. 37 and 46); Prof. J. S. Hoyland and Messrs The Challenge, Ltd. (for the prayer on p. 71); to the Rev. L. S. Hunter (for use of four lines from a hymn by the late Dr John Hunter on p. 20); to Miss L. Hensley (for use of eight lines of a hymn by Lewis Hensley on p. 65); to Mr Rudyard Kipling and Messrs Macmillan & Co. (for four lines of a hymn from "The Children's Song" in "Puck of Pook's Hill" on p. 61).

Grateful acknowledgment is also made of the great help obtained from *Great Souls at Prayer* and *A Chain of Prayer Across the Ages* in compiling this book. If any copyright has been unwittingly infringed, apologies are offered. In some cases the borrowed prayers have been slightly altered.

Sources of Borrowed Prayers (marked thus *)—

On Page 13—*Anthology of Prayers for Public Worship*.
,,   ,,   13—St Ignatius Loyola.
,,   ,,   15—Christina G. Rossetti.
,,   ,,   19—B. F. Westcott.
,,   ,,   29—Nicholas Ridley (Martyr, 1555).
,,   ,,   31—*Gelasian Sacramentary*.
,,   ,,   32—Archbishop Randall Davidson.
,,   ,,   35—Bishop Thomas Wilson.
,,   ,,   37—*A Book of Prayers for Students* (S.C.M.).
,,   ,,   43—Henry Alford.
,,   ,,   45—*Gelasian Sacramentary*.
,,   ,,   46—*A Book of Prayers for Students* (S.C.M.).
,,   ,,   50—*Mozarabic Liturgy*.
,,   ,,   55—*Mozarabic Liturgy*.
,,   ,,   59—Christina G. Rossetti.
,,   ,,   63—Christina G. Rossetti.
,,   ,,   67—*Treasury of Devotion*.
,,   ,,   71—J. S. Hoyland.

ABOUT THE USE OF THIS BOOK

WHY USE SUCH A BOOK?—It is meant to help you to learn how to pray. Now perhaps you think that so long as you are young you need not take that part of your religion very seriously. You would rather follow Christ in a more active and "open-air" kind of way. Well, yes: have an active and "open-air" kind of Christianity by all means. But it wouldn't be at all like the Christianity of Christ if we left prayer out: there can be no mistake about that. It may be difficult for you to find times and places for solitary prayer. But Jesus Himself had just that difficulty, and He found a way out, because He could not do without prayer (see Matt. xiv. 22, 23; Mark i. 32-38; Luke vi. 12, 13; John vii. 53-viii. 1). His way out was, quite literally, an "open-air" way. Perhaps you will find that way useful too. But in any case if *He* could not do without prayer, and spoke so much about it to His disciples, are we going to try to do without it? No, if you are in earnest about following Him you will make up your mind to begin at once a regular habit of finding time for private devotion. It will be difficult at first to keep to it, but you can do it if you make up your mind, and then it will become natural.

But, to come closer to the point: even when you have made up your mind and secured your time for prayer, you may feel at first that you hardly know what to do with it. You know that it is not enough to keep repeating a prayer you learnt by heart when you were a child. But when you try to go beyond that and pray to God for yourself, perhaps you feel that you hardly know *how* to pray; or at least you could begin to carry out

7

your resolution more faithfully if you had something definite, each day, on which to begin. Well, that is just where this little book is meant to help you.

How to Use the Book.—It contains daily devotions for four weeks. Take it, in your quiet time each day, as you kneel down (that seems to be the posture that, as a rule, helps us most to concentrate our thoughts in prayer). Open it at the page for the day, and go through the day's portion. First come the words from the Bible, on the subject of the day, to set your thoughts right at the start. When you come to the prayers remember that they *are prayers*, and that you are not simply to read them through, but to pray them, really speaking from your heart to God. You will find on the pages also not only fully worded prayers, but *suggestions*, that you should work out in your own way, as to the kind of things you might pray about; because the important matter is that we should learn to pray to God *ourselves*, about our *own* needs, and our *own* friends, and so on. Sometimes also you will find, printed in different type, a few words of guidance to help you to *think* quietly of the subject for the day in relation to your own life.

Don't try to race through the day's portion simply for the sake of getting it read; and still more, don't allow yourself to waste time reading it over mechanically with your mind wandering. It is a good thing sometimes to pause and try to realise God's presence, so as to make sure we are really praying. Two minutes of real prayer are worth more than ten minutes of half-hearted prayer; and if your time is short it is better to take a *bit* of the day's portion and go through it thoughtfully than to hurry through the whole of it.

The Lord's Prayer is not printed on any of the daily pages, but once for all on a page by itself at the beginning of the book, because it must always have a place by itself in the devotions of Christian people. This does not mean that you

should not use it often, but just the opposite—
that you *should*. Of course you know it by heart,
and do not need to have it on each page. But
just because you know it so well it is very easy
to repeat it *mechanically* ; and it is all the more
necessary to stop and think of its petitions, and
to make sure you know and mean what you are
saying. Try to connect its familiar phrases with
some of the things you want to pray about—your
worries about to-morrow, your temptations, the
people whom you find it hard to forgive.

PAGES FOR SPECIAL OCCASIONS will be found
towards the end of the book. Look at them now
and see what the occasions are, and then you will
remember to turn to them when the times come.

THE BLANK PAGES at the end are put there that
you may note down for yourself anything that you
may specially wish to remember and use : things
you wish to pray about from time to time, or any
thoughts or prayers from Scripture or anywhere
else that you think will be of help to you. The
INTERLEAVED EDITION gives still further opportunity for this. Everyone may not find this method
helpful ; but if you do use it, it will make the book
much more your own.

ABOUT READING THE BIBLE.—It is obviously
not enough to read, time after time, the Scripture
passages that are printed in full on the daily pages.
So you will find on the page, each day, references
to about half a dozen other passages bearing on
the day's subject. If you turn to these in your
Bible, one at a time, taking a different one each
time you come round to that page in successive
months, you will cover more ground. But of
course you will not be content to confine your
Bible reading to this tiny selection, but will find
your way about the Bible for yourself. Try the
Revised Version as well as the Authorised, and also
some modern translation like Weymouth's or
Moffatt's, especially for the New Testament. You
will find them illuminating.

ABOUT THE LIMITS OF THIS BOOK.—No book of prayers can ever take the place of the prayers that should rise from our own hearts, and this book would not be serving its purpose well if the people who begin using it were to keep on using it for ever as their one and only aid to devotion. When you have used it for a while it will perhaps make you wish to pass on to some other such book, and there are many that may help you. But it will be serving its purpose best of all if it helps you to learn to pray to God for yourself, and so to discover something of the strength and joy and cleansing that men and women of all generations have found, for themselves and others, in their times of prayer.

The following list of books may be useful.

A Chain of Prayer Across the Ages.
    Ed. S. E. Fox. (Murray, 5s.)
Great Souls at Prayer.
    Ed. M. W. Tileston. (Allenson, 3s. 6d.)
The Meaning of Prayer.
    By H. E. Fosdick. (S.C.M., 3s. 6d.)
A Book of Prayers for Students.
    (S.C.M., 3s. 6d.)
Private Prayers for Young Men and Women.
    A. B. Macaulay. (Hodder & Stoughton, 3s. 6d.)
The New Testament in Modern Speech.
    R. F. Weymouth. (Clarke & Co., 3s. 9d.)
The New Testament: A New Translation.
    Moffatt. (Hodder & Stoughton, 4s. 6d.)

THE LORD'S PRAYER

OUR FATHER WHICH ART IN HEAVEN,
HALLOWED BE THY NAME.
THY KINGDOM COME.
THY WILL BE DONE ON EARTH, AS IT IS
IN HEAVEN.
GIVE US THIS DAY OUR DAILY BREAD.
AND FORGIVE US OUR DEBTS, AS WE FORGIVE
OUR DEBTORS.
AND LEAD US NOT INTO TEMPTATION,
BUT DELIVER US FROM EVIL:
FOR THINE IS THE KINGDOM,
AND THE POWER,
AND THE GLORY,
FOR EVER.   AMEN.

OUR DEBT TO CHRIST

" God so loved the world that He gave His only begotten Son, that whosoever believeth on Him should not perish, but have eternal life."—John iii. 16.

" The Son of God, Who loved me and gave Himself for me."—Gal. ii. 20.

Other Readings : Luke vii. 36-47 ; 2 Cor. v. 14-19 ; Eph. iii. 14-21 ; Phil. ii. 5-11 ; 1 Tim. i. 12-17 ; Rev. i. 4-6.

Think of how much Jesus suffered for us : how He was deserted by friends, condemned unjustly, scourged, nailed to the Cross ; how He endured hours of agony, and finally suffered death itself, with great public shame, and what seemed the most complete and tragic failure. Think of how in this great sacrificing love we see the very love of God Himself. Remember that this love is still calling you to be His child, forgiving your sins and failures, and helping you against them by His spirit in your heart. Take time now to give thanks. . . .

Thou, O Christ, art my Lord and Saviour. I trust in Thee. Thanks be unto God for His unspeakable gift.

Let me ask that Christ may be the centre of all my living.

> Christ be with me, Christ within me,
> Christ behind me, Christ before me,
> Christ beside me, Christ to win me,
> Christ to comfort and restore me,
> Christ beneath me, Christ above me,
> Christ in quiet, Christ in danger,
> Christ in hearts of all that love me,
> Christ in mouth of friend and stranger.

A Prayer for Love to Christ

Blessed Lord, may we cherish the remembrance of all that Thou hast done and suffered for us, and of all that Thou hast promised to be to those who trust in Thee. O that we may love Thee, Who hast so loved us! May Thy love constrain us to give ourselves wholly to Thee, for in loving Thee there is perpetual joy and strength. Enable us to attain a clearer vision of things unseen and eternal. Grant that every aspiration breathed into our souls this day by Thy Holy Spirit may endure, so that we may rise to higher things in the days that are to come.*

Heavenly Father, help me to go to Thy worship this day with a deep sense of all Thou hast done for me through Jesus Christ. Bless all who this day are meeting together to remember Thy love, and all who are seeking to spread the knowledge of it in the world. Bless those who do not know Thy love, and those who care nothing for it.

If there are any whom I find it hard to love and to forgive, let me think of them now with charity and with humility, as I remember how much I myself depend on the great pardoning love of God. . . .

Forgive us our debts, as we forgive our debtors.

A Dedication

Teach us, good Lord, to serve Thee as Thou deservest; to give and not to count the cost; to fight and not to heed the wounds; to toil and not to seek for rest; to labour and not to ask for any reward save that of knowing that we do Thy will; through Jesus Christ our Lord. Amen.*

13

THE SERVICE OF MAN

" You know the so-called rulers of the Gentiles lord
     it over them,
And their great men overbear them :
     not so with you.
Whoever wants to be great among you must be
     your servant,
and whoever of you wants to be first must be
     your slave ;
for the Son of man himself has not come to be
     served but to serve,
and to give His life as a ransom for many."
Mark x. 42-45.   (Moffatt.)

Other Readings : Lev. xix. 9-18 ; 1 Kings iii.
5-10 ; Luke x. 30-37 ; Luke xxii. 24-27 ; John xxi.
15-19 ; Acts xx. 17-24.

*" The greatest thing a man can do for his
Heavenly Father is to be kind to some of His other
children." I want to make the most of my life.
Am I going about it in the right way? Jesus
taught by His words, His life, and His death, that
the greatest thing any man can do is to forget himself and serve others. Great opportunities of service
may not come at once to everybody, but if we are
filled with the love of God we shall be sensitive,
as Jesus was, to the needs of others. Remember
the lines about*

That best portion of a good man's life,
His little, nameless, unremembered acts
Of kindness and of love.

Thou hast been kind to me, O Father, and I
acknowledge all the gracious gifts of Thy love.
(*Be silent, and name the blessings that have made glad
your heart.*) . . . Now I know that Thou hast
blessed me, and Thou would'st have me share these
blessings with others. Forgive my selfish ways.

14

Help me so to love Thee that with a happy heart I may be kinder to my loved ones at home ; to my companions ; to those who forget to be kind to me ; to all whose burdens are heavier than mine. Help me to live my daily life and do my work as a willing service. Help me to keep myself ever fit in body and soul, that I may be ready to accept any special service to which Thou wilt call me. This I ask in the Name of Him who loved and served His fellows even unto death.

INTERCESSION

Let me remember the poor, and all who are seeking to be their helpers and to banish poverty from the world. . . .

Let me remember the men and women whose daily toil is costly service (missionaries, miners, nurses, soldiers, sailors, all engaged in dangerous occupations). . . .

Let me remember social reformers, peacemakers, and all who are seeking to deliver the captives of evil from their chains. . . .

O Lord, Creator of all things, be gracious, I entreat Thee, unto all Thy creatures. Give us all grace to serve Thee in our appointed place, rejoicing before Thee to Thy praise ; each fulfilling the law under which Thou bringest him, each glorifying Thee according to the special excellence Thou bestowest. Amen.*

GOD AND MY MOODS

" Why art thou cast down, O my soul ? and why art thou disquieted within me ? hope in God : for I shall yet praise Him, Who is the health of my countenance, and my God."—Psalm, xliii. 5.

" But we have this treasure in earthen vessels, that the excellency of the power may be of God, and not of us. We are troubled on every side, yet not distressed ; we are perplexed, but not in despair; persecuted, but not forsaken; cast down, but not destroyed ; always bearing about in the body the dying of the Lord Jesus, that the life also of Jesus might be made manifest in our body. For we which live are alway delivered unto death for Jesus' sake, that the life also of Jesus might be made manifest in our mortal flesh."—2 Cor. iv. 7-11.

Other Readings : 1 Kings xix. 4-8 ; Psalm xlii. 1-5; Psalm cii. 25-28; Jonah iv. ; Rom. viii. 24-28 ; 2 Cor. vii. 5, 6.

An Act of Penitence.

Think of the misery we cause ourselves and others by uncontrolled bad moods ; by fits of depression in which opportunities are lost ; by moods of sullenness and resentment in which cruel things are said and done. Examine yourself for such failures, and for the causes of them—neglect of health ; neglect of prayer ; wounded pride which will neither own a fault nor accept forgiveness ; obstinacy ; selfishness.

O God, Who art greater than my heart and knowest all things, I confess how uncertain and weak my life is, yielding feebly to each passing mood, making no brave fight, and forgetting to pray. I have allowed my moods to spoil the lives of those around me, and make their battle harder. Give me grace now to turn away from these sins, and to enter into Thy peace.

A MEDITATION

Think quietly of the faithfulness of God " Who slumbers not nor sleeps." He is without respect of persons. He makes the sun to rise on the evil and the good, and sends rain on the just and the unjust. In all His dealings with us He has a steadfast purpose of love. Through all the changes of our changing lives He does not change. He keeps them in perfect peace whose minds are stayed on Him.

A PRAYER

Eternal Father, strong to save, I seek to come near to Thee through Jesus Christ, Whose presence is peace. I bless Thee for Thy faithfulness, and pray for help in every time of inconstancy. May I yield my life now to Thy saving power, that through Thy strength this day I may conquer and not be conquered. I ask this not only for myself but for all who are fighting bravely to be cheerful, some ill and weak in body, some tempted to give way to angry or despondent moods. Grant, O God, that by the example of my joy and courage I may help others to trust in Thee. Through Jesus Christ Our Lord. Amen.

I grasp Thy strength, make it mine own,
My heart with peace is blest ;
I lose my hold, and then comes down
  Darkness and cold unrest.
Let me no more my comfort draw
From my frail hold of Thee ;
In this alone rejoice with awe—
  Thy mighty grasp of me.

TRUTHFULNESS

" And this is the message which we have heard from Him, and announce unto you, that God is light, and in Him is no darkness at all. If we say that we have fellowship with Him, and walk in the darkness, we lie, and do not the truth : but if we walk in the light, as He is in the light, we have fellowship one with another, and the blood of Jesus His Son cleanseth us from all sin. If we say that we have no sin, we deceive ourselves, and the truth is not in us. If we confess our sins, He is faithful and righteous to forgive us our sins, and to cleanse us from all unrighteousness.—1 John i. 5-9.

Other Readings : 2 Kings v. 20-27 ; Psalm xv. ; Luke xi. 34-44 ; John viii. 26-32 ; John xiv. 15-26 ; 1 Thess. v. 5-23 ; Hymn 172.

O God, Who hast called us out of darkness into Thy marvellous light, with all Thy people I would thank Thee for Jesus Christ, the Light of the World. Give me perseverance to seek Him, insight to recognise Him, love to obey Him.

Meditate for a few minutes upon Jesus as we see Him in the Gospels—His utter faithfulness in word and deed to His knowledge of God ; His directness and simplicity in dealing with men, which quietly penetrated their pretences and defences ; the straightness and kindness of His rebukes ; His silences ; the perfect truthfulness and sincerity which made Him always a disturber of darkness and a rallying-point of truth. As these things move us to love and admiration, His spirit is already at work in our hearts, preparing us for meeting God in prayer.

18

" If we say, ' we are not guilty,' we are deceiving ourselves ! "

Let me confess my common sins against the truth as it is in Jesus. Have I concealed the best that is in me ? Have I uttered falsehood, or consented to it by silence ? Do I unduly love to be praised ? Do I resent just rebuke or criticism, blaming others when the fault is really my own ? Do I sometimes speak " plain truths " uncharitably, without being sure of the sincerity and kindness of my motives ? I will resolve before God to renounce these sins.

O Thou that searchest the hearts of men, look with mercy upon these my sins against Thy truth ; forgive them for Jesus' sake ; and help me to walk in the light this day. Deliver me from timid or sullen silence ; give me grace to speak with simple truth and open kindness ; and so dwell in my heart by Thy Spirit of Truth that thought, word and deed may be made one in love.

Almighty God, Who hast sent the Spirit of Truth unto us to guide us into all truth, so rule our lives by Thy power that we may be truthful in word, deed and thought. O keep us, most merciful Saviour, with Thy gracious protection, that no fear or hope may ever make us false in act or speech. Cast out from us whatsoever loveth or maketh a lie, and bring us all to the perfect freedom of Thy truth ; through Jesus Christ Thy Son our Lord. Amen.*

Let me remember before God all who serve the cause of truth—ministers and teachers, who serve truth with their lips . . .; writers of books and newspapers, who serve truth with their pens. . . .

Let the words of my mouth and the meditation of my heart be acceptable in Thy sight, O Lord, my Strength and my Redeemer. Amen.

HOME

" Is not this the carpenter's son ? Is not His mother called Mary ? And His brethren James, and Joses, and Simon, and Judas ? And His sisters, are they not all with us ? "—Matt. xiii. 55, 56.

" Love is very patient, very kind. Love knows no jealousy ; love makes no parade, gives itself no airs, is never rude, never selfish, never irritated, never resentful ; love is never glad when others go wrong, love is gladdened by goodness, always slow to expose, always eager to believe the best, always hopeful, always patient."—1 Cor. xiii. 4-8. (Moffatt.)

Other Readings : Matt. xviii. 1-6 ; Matt. xix. 13-15 ; John xix. 25-27 ; 2 Tim. ii. 19-24 ; 1 John iv. 7-12 ; 1 John iv. 20, 21.

> *Read slowly these verses from 1 Cor. xiii., and try to picture the carpenter's home in Nazareth when " Love Incarnate, Love Divine " was dwelling in it. Remember that Jesus lived the greater part of his life in that home, working for it, and serving His Father perfectly in it. Remember, too, that He went out from it when the call came to a larger service, and that He said, " Who is My mother? and who are My brethren? . . . whosoever shall do the will of My Father Which is in heaven, the same is My brother, and sister, and mother."*

> Dear Master, in whose life I see
> All that I would but fail to be,
> Let Thy clear light for ever shine,
> To shame and guide this life of mine.

Remember the ways by which God has blessed your life through your home, and give thanks :

O God, Who hast taught us to call Thee Father, I thank Thee that Thou hast set Thy children in families. I thank Thee for my own home ; for the joy and strength that have come to my life through home ; for the love and sacrifice of parents ; for the comradeship of brothers and sisters.

Hear me now as I ask Thy blessing for the members of my own family, and bring before Thee the needs of each as they are known to me. . . . (Naming each.)

O Thou Who art the Father of all, I pray Thee for the homeless ; for those who have never known the joy of home ; for those who have wandered far from the homes of their childhood. I ask Thy pity and mercy for all whose homes have been made unhappy through their own folly or the sins of others. May the homes of our nation be set free from impurity; from intemperance; from gambling; from foolish luxury. May they find their true joy in the love of Thee and the rule of Christ. I ask it in His Name.

Consider the ways in which you have failed in the home : through being more ready to accept its comforts and affection than to share in its work and cares ; through impatience, bad-temper and selfishness ; through making unreasonable demands on the service of others ; through blindness to the needs of parents, brothers and sisters ; through giving them less than their share of love, understanding and companionship.

Father, I bring to Thee with shame and penitence these my failures in my home. Forgive me for them. Hear and strengthen me in the promises I now make before Thee. . . . (Set before yourself now particular ways in which you may to-day bring the love of God into your own home and the homes of others.)

SUFFERING

" Surely He hath borne our griefs, and carried our sorrows ; yet we did esteem Him stricken, smitten of God, and afflicted. But He was wounded for our transgressions, He was bruised for our iniquities, the chastisement of our peace was upon Him, and with His stripes we are healed."—Isa. liii. 4-5.

" In all these things we are more than conquerors through Him that loved us."—Rom. viii. 37.

Other Readings : Deut. viii. 1-6 ; Matt. viii. 14-17 ; Mark xiv. 32-36 ; 2 Cor. xii. 7-10 ; 2 Tim. ii. 7-13 ; Heb. xii. 3-11.

SEED-THOUGHTS FOR MEDITATION

The best man that ever lived was the most joy-ful, and He also had the greatest experience of suffering. . . .
It is right to escape from suffering, and to help others to escape, unless love and honour forbid. . . .
When suffering is unavoidable it is right to bear it bravely and cheerfully, and to keep on hoping for relief. . . .
When we suffer through our own wrong-doing, we ought to bear it humbly, gratefully, and turn away from the sin that has caused it. . . .
When we suffer through the sins of others it is Christlike to endure quietly, and to return good for evil. . . .
God can bring good out of evil, especially through the brave faith of the sufferer, as He did so wonderfully in the case of the Cross of Jesus Christ. . . .
Many men and women have only come to know God intimately through the experience of suffer-ing. . . .

My God, I thank Thee, who hast made
    The earth so bright,
So full of splendour and of joy,
    Beauty and light ;
So many glorious things are here,
    Noble and right.

I thank Thee more that all our joy
    Is touched with pain,
That shadows fall on brightest hours,
    That thorns remain,
So that earth's bliss may be our guide,
    And not our chain.

O God, Whose mercy is over all Thy works, forgive me for every pain that I have caused to Thee and to the children of Thy love through ignorance, through thoughtlessness, and especially through wilful sin and selfishness. . . .

Save me from dullness of feeling and hardness of heart. Make me quick to notice, and eager to relieve the pains and sorrows of others.

Give me courage, hope and patience under trial. Lead me day by day more deeply into the secret of the love that suffers long and still is kind. Help me to take up my cross and follow Christ ; and may the light from His Cross transfigure mine.

O Father, Who dost not willingly afflict nor grieve the children of men, hear my prayer for the sufferers and sad people around me ; for the victims of injustice and cruelty ; for all who are finding that the way of transgressors is hard. . . .

Especially I ask Thy divine compassion and aid for. . . . These things I ask in the Name of Him Who endured the Cross for the joy that was set before Him. Amen.

23

GOD IN NATURE

" O Lord, our Lord,
How excellent is Thy name in all the earth !
Who hast set Thy glory upon the heavens. . . .
When I consider Thy heavens, the work of Thy
    fingers,
The moon and the stars which Thou hast ordained ;
What is man, that Thou art mindful of him ?
And the son of man, that Thou visitest him ? "

Psalm viii. 1, 3, 4.

" Consider the lilies of the field, how they grow ;
they toil not neither do they spin : yet I say unto
you that even Solomon in all his glory was not
arrayed like one of these. But if God doth so
clothe the grass of the field . . . ."—Matt. vi. 28-30.

Other Readings: Gen. i. ; Psalm civ. 16-35 ;
Psalm cxlviii. ; Isa. xl. 12-26 ; Mark iv. 26-32 ;
Rev. xxii. 1-5.

THANKSGIVING

For the wonderful story of the world being
brought out of chaos through countless ages,
for Jesus Christ who saw the Father's hand in
the ways of nature,
for all the beauty of earth and sky and sea, for
sunshine and wind and rain, for the starry heavens
by night, for the peace of country places, for hills
and woods and streams, for birds and flowers and
all the wonder of living things,
    I give Thee, O heavenly Father, my glad
    thanks.

Thou who hast given me eyes to see
    And love this sight so fair,
Give me a heart to find out Thee,
    And read Thee everywhere.

24

Make me, O God, more worthy of such beauty and bounty.

> If I have enjoyed it with an impure heart,
>
> if I have been sullen and fretful, or mean and covetous, in the midst of it,
>
> if I have lived an unbeautiful life in Thy beautiful world,

help me sincerely to repent; forgive me; cleanse and save me. Make me, O Heavenly Father, a true follower, day by day, of Him in Whom the Word was made flesh and dwelt among men. So may I learn to look with pure and reverent eyes upon all Thy creation, and glorify Thee daily in my body and my spirit which are Thine.

INTERCESSION

O Thou faithful and loving Creator, look in pity upon those who cannot enjoy the beauty of Thy world: those long confined in sick-rooms (especially . . .); those who live in dark places, with little sunshine and little beauty; those who have no sight, and those whom worldly care has made blind to the beauty around them.

Bless and help all those lovers of mankind who seek to bring beauty into the lives of their fellows.

> And hasten, Lord, that perfect day
> When pain and death shall cease,
> And Thy just rule shall fill the earth
> With health and light and peace;
> When ever blue the sky shall gleam,
> And ever green the sod,
> And man's rude work deface no more
> The paradise of God.

THE CHURCH OF CHRIST

" As the human body is one and has many
members, all the members of the body forming
one body for all their number, so is it with Christ.
For by one Spirit we have all been baptised into
one Body, Jews or Greeks, slaves or freemen ; we
have all been imbued with one Spirit. . . . If one
member suffers, all the members share its suffering ; if one member is honoured, all the members
share its honour.   Now you are Christ's Body, and
severally members of it."—1 Cor. xii. 12, 13, 26, 27.
(Moffatt.)

Other Readings : Matt. xvi. 13-19 ; Acts ii. 41-47 ;
Acts iv. 23-37 ; Rom. xii. 4-15 ; Eph. iv. 4-16 ;
Col. i. 9-24.

*Think for a moment of the Church as " the Body
of Christ."   That means that through His Church
Christ still walks about the world, and speaks to
people, and lays His hand on them to bless them.*

THANKSGIVING

Eternal Father, Who hast called me into the
fellowship of the Church of Thy dear Son, with
the whole company of Thy people in Heaven and
earth I worship and adore Thee.

I praise Thee for the long story of the Church
through all the centuries ;
> for the countless host of those who have borne
> its burdens ;
> for the countless host of those who have been
> saved and helped through its influence ;
> for its brave missionary enterprise in all the
> world ;
> for the joy and strength I have found in its
> worship ;
> for those who gave me to Thee in the Sacra-
> ment of Baptism, and all who since then have
> helped me to grow up as Thy child ;

26

For those who started Youth Cooperation

for the help Thou givest in the Sacrament of
the Lord's Supper;
for any service I have been able to do in the
Church, and for the friendship and strength
and light that have come to me in the doing
of it.

CONFESSION

I confess unto Thee, O Lord, with shame and
penitence, the sins of Thy Church, and especially
my own share in them; our lack of courage to
bear witness to Christ and to do His will; our
jealousies and hypocrisies; our loveless and un-
believing hearts when we come to worship Thee.
Forgive us, O God, and fill us with the brave,
believing, loving spirit of our Lord and Master.

INTERCESSION

Think quietly now of your own congregation,
its worship and its work to-day, and ask God to
bless it. . . . If there is any part of its work in
which you are specially concerned, or any of its
people for whom you specially want God's help,
pray for them now (the children you teach in
Sunday School . . . those who work with you
in some organisation . . . or sing with you in the
choir . . .). Think also of the wonderful world-
wide Church of Christ to which you belong, and
pray for it.
O Lord our God, help us all this day to worship
Thee in spirit and in truth, and to serve Thee
with freedom and with power. May we be as Thy
family, united to love and serve Thee. Bless Thy
Church everywhere. And especially in those lands
where it is young and struggling amid ancient
ignorance and superstition, do Thou encourage and
help Thy missionary servants, and through them
bless Thy world.
Now unto Him that is able to do exceeding
abundantly above all that we ask or think, according to the power that worketh in us, unto Him be
glory in the Church and in Christ Jesus throughout
all ages, world without end. Amen.

COURAGE

" Hast thou not known, hast thou not heard, that the everlasting God, the Lord, the Creator of the ends of the earth, fainteth not, neither is weary ? there is no searching of His understanding. He giveth power to the faint ; and to them that have no might He increaseth strength."—Isaiah xl. 28, 29.

" But after long abstinence Paul stood forth in the midst of them, and said, Sirs . . . I exhort you to be of good cheer . . . for there stood by me this night the angel of God, Whose I am, and Whom I serve, saying, Fear not, Paul. . . . Wherefore, sirs, be of good cheer : for I believe God, that it shall be even as it was told me. . . ."—Acts xxvii. 21-25.

Other Readings : Josh. i. 1-9 ; Psalm xxvii. 1-6 ; Dan. vi. 4-10 ; Matt. x. 16-31 ; Mark iv. 35-41 ; Acts iv. 13-20 ; Hymn 528 ; Hymn 537.

Let your mind dwell quietly for a while upon " the everlasting God, the Lord, the Creator of the ends of the earth," Who is revealed to us in Jesus Christ. What God was for Isaiah and Paul, that He is for you in every hour of to-day.

I bind unto myself to-day
The power of God to hold and lead,
His eye to watch, His might to stay,
His ear to hearken to my need ;
The wisdom of my God to teach,
His hand to guide, His shield to ward,
The word of God to give me speech,
His heavenly host to be my guard.

Think now of the particular calls for courage in to-day's journey so far as you can foresee it : physical courage ; the courage of your convictions ;
28

*the courage of initiative, making a new start, taking
the lead where others stand back ; the courage of
perseverance ; the courage of resistance :*

(*" And then he bit his lips, clenching the mind,
  And staggered out to muster, beating back
The coward frozen self of him that whined.
  Come what cards might, he meant to play
  the pack."*)

*O God and Father of our Lord Jesus Christ, I
thank Thee for His glorious example of Manhood ;
for His courage in the storm ; for His brave can-
dour and scorn of consequence when truth and
love were at stake ; for His endurance of the Cross ;
for His faith in Thy Kingdom. O Lord Who
knowest all my faintheartedness, my profitless
gloom and anxiety, and all the hidden motions of
fear in my spirit, help me this day to strive, to
venture, and to endure, as a good soldier of Jesus
Christ. This I ask in His Name. Amen.

Think now of the need of others for encouragement.

Pray for worried, nervous, and timid people
. . .; races bound by superstitious fear, who have
never heard of Christ . . .; those haunted by the
fears that grow from unforgiven sins. . . . Offer
yourself to be used by God to encourage others as
you may have opportunity to-day. . . .

O Heavenly Father, the Father of all wisdom,
understanding and true strength, we beseech Thee
to look mercifully upon Thy servants, and send
Thy Holy Spirit into their hearts, that when they
must join to fight in the field for the glory of Thy
holy Name, then they, being strengthened by the
defence of Thy right hand, may manfully stand
in the confession of Thy faith and of Thy truth,
and continue in the same unto the end of their
lives, through Jesus Christ our Lord. Amen.*

MY READING

" Finally, brethren, whatsoever things are true, whatsoever things are honest, whatsoever things are just, whatsoever things are pure, whatsoever things are lovely, whatsoever things are of good report ; if there be any virtue, and if there be any praise, think on these things."—Phil. iv. 8.

Other Readings : Psalm xix. ; Psalm cxix. 9-16 ; Prov. iii. 13-20 ; 2 Tim. iii. 14-17 ; Heb. i. 1-4 ; Hymn 202 ; Hymn 503.

Why do we read ? For enjoyment ? for the love of beauty ? for knowledge ? to understand life and to manage it well ? What would Christ think of your reading ? Is most of it light and commonplace ? is it childish ? is there much real beauty and truth and joy in it ? is it clean ? is it feeding, or starving, or poisoning your mind ? Are you really making use of the wonderful privilege of being able to read and having such a wealth of good reading within your reach in this modern world ?

THANKSGIVING

Eternal God, Giver of all goodness, beauty and truth, I praise Thee for these Thy gifts, to which Thou openest men's eyes in age after age, and with the love of which Thou enlargest their hearts. I praise Thee, I bless Thee, I adore Thee, for Thy Word made flesh in Jesus. I praise Thee for Thy gift of the Bible, speaking to us of Thee and of Him who is Thy Son. I praise Thee for its coming to us in our native tongue, through the labours and struggles of Thy brave servants in bygone days. I praise Thee for all strength and cheer, light and cleansing, that I have found in its words. I praise Thee, O my God, for all good and beautiful books. I praise Thee for enriching my leisure hours with

30

them, giving me wisdom and joy, solemn thought and wholesome laughter, all from Thy hand.

CONFESSION

For neglect of Thy Word ; for indifference to the story of Jesus Christ ; for heedlessness to Thy voice ;
    Forgive me, O God.
For all foolishness in my reading ; for indolence in the quest of what is true and good ; for misuse of Thy gifts, in reading what is evil ;
    Forgive me, O God.
Give me, O Heavenly Father, insight and perseverance in the love of what Thou lovest. Strengthen me to put away whatsoever would turn my heart to evil, and to seek, in all my reading, the things that are true and lovely and of good report.

INTERCESSION

O Lord our God, Who callest us to be true stewards of all Thy gifts, hear my prayer now—
    for all who with their pen influence the lives of men and women . . . all writers, editors, journalists . . .
    for those who make books—publishers and printers—that by their craft they may honour Thee . . .
    for all who print and circulate the Bible, in any language, in this and other lands. . . .

May the entrance of Thy Word give light in all the world.

O Thou Who art the Light of the minds that know Thee, the Life of the souls that love Thee, and the Strength of the thoughts that seek Thee ; help us so to know Thee that we may truly love Thee, so to love Thee that we may fully serve Thee, Whose service is perfect freedom ; through Jesus Christ our Lord.   Amen.*

CITIZENSHIP

" God be merciful unto us and bless us, and cause His face to shine upon us; that Thy way may be known upon earth, Thy saving health among all nations. Let the people praise Thee, O God; let all the people praise Thee. O let the nations be glad and sing for joy: for Thou shalt judge the people righteously and govern the nations upon earth."—Psalm lxvii. 1-4.

Other Readings: Psalm lxxii. 12-19; Psalm cii. 13-22; Isa. lxii.; Mark x. 42-45; 1 Pet. ii. 13-17; Rev. xxi. 1-4; Hymn 647.

THANKSGIVING

I thank Thee, O Father, for my country; for its history; for its love of freedom; for its heritage of faith; for its heroes and martyrs who have stood for what is good and right; for all the privileges which are mine by being born in this land; for every fine impulse stirred in my blood by its glory and its shame.

Remember that God gives you His gifts, not for your good only, but to enable you to serve your day and generation. You are not here to live for yourself, but to help, to be used, to contribute your share, great or small, to the common good.

INTERCESSION

Pray for the King, for all who have special responsibility in governing this country, in making or administering its laws, in guiding its public life.

O God Almighty, guide our Sovereign and all those to whom Thou hast committed the government of our nation and empire; and grant to them special gifts of wisdom and understanding, of counsel and strength, that, upholding what is right and following what is true, they may obey Thy holy will and fulfil Thy divine purpose.*

Bring before God the sins and needs of your country, as you know them.
Pray for the men and women who have forgotten God, and little children who have never known Him;
>   for homes made unhappy by drink, gambling and impurity;
>   for your fellow-citizens who live in houses where health and happiness seem impossible;
>   for those who cannot find work.

Eternal Father, Who hast commanded us to bear one another's burdens, grant that I may be swift to feel the needs of others and to consult their interests in all I do, so that as I do my work, as I enjoy my pleasures, as I use my vote, I may know the Spirit of Jesus Christ. May I be a true citizen daily among my fellows upon earth, because Thou hast made me a citizen of Thine unseen and glorious Kingdom.

A PRAYER

O God our King, Who hast called us through Jesus Christ to be kings and priests unto Thee, teach us all to bear one another's burdens and the burdens of the commonwealth, with Thy royal law of love in our hearts, and the sacrificial spirit of our great High Priest Jesus Christ. Give us all, I beseech Thee, a wounding vision of the woes of this our land, the misery of the slums, the despair in the lives of many of our fellow-citizens, the wan faces of little children, the deep and shameful wrongs waiting to be put right. Give us also a vision of our land as Thou wouldst have it be, and as Thou by Thy love in the hearts of Thy servants canst remake it. And take us to be Thy servants, giving us no rest or discharge until Thou hast wrought this work of pity: that generations yet unborn may praise Thy Name; through Christ our Lord. Amen.

TEMPTATION

" I cannot understand my own actions ; I do not act as I want to act ; on the contrary, I do what I detest . . . the wish is there, but not the power of doing what is right. I cannot be as good as I want to be, and I do wrong against my wishes. . . . I want to do what is right, but wrong is all I can manage ; I cordially agree with God's law, so far as my inner self is concerned, but then I find quite another law in my members which conflicts with the law of my mind and makes me a prisoner to sin's law that resides in my members. . . . Miserable wretch that I am ! Who will rescue me from this body of death ? God will ! Thanks be to Him through Jesus Christ our Lord."—Rom. vii. 15-25. (Moffatt.)

Other Readings : Matt. iv. 1-11 ; Luke xxii. 28-34 ; 1 Cor. x. 11-13 ; Gal. vi. 7-10 ; Heb. iv. 14-16 ; James i. 12-17.

Do you find your besetting sins returning so often that you almost despair of ever getting rid of them ? Do you even sometimes accept them miserably as part of yourself ? But that is the way of defeat ; and, as Paul discovered through Christ, God means us to live victoriously.

First, then, set before yourself the ways in which you fall into your besetting sins : through concentration upon yourself, the wish to be thought clever by others, slackness about your thoughts and desires, through books, pictures, companions. . . .
And now turn in prayer to God.

Our thoughts lie open to Thy sight,
    And naked to Thy glance.
Our secret sins are in the light
    Of Thy pure countenance.

Heavenly Father, I confess with shame how often in thought and word and deed I have yielded to evil without seeking Thy help to resist.

Forgive me, Lord, for my poor fighting, and teach me the secret of victory.

Now remember with joy and thanksgiving how hosts of men and women in all ages have chosen to suffer rather than turn from the path of duty : most of all, Jesus Christ Himself ; and then the " noble army of martyrs " ; and all the unknown people who set their teeth and go straight when tempted to take an easier way ; all those who " out of weakness were made strong " by looking to God.

O Lord my God, ever faithful and kind, Thou wilt not suffer me to be tempted beyond my strength if I will but look to Thee. Teach me to look to Thee every day. Keep me this day in the light of Thy presence. Make Thy glory so real to me that temptation will lose its power. And bind my heart to what is pure and true, that I may never forsake or betray it for any gain or pleasure, but all my life long be brave and clean and kind. Be Thou my strength. This I ask through Him Who was tempted in all points like ourselves, yet without sin, Jesus Christ our Lord.

INTERCESSION

Pray for all who are suffering fierce temptation to-day, that God will be their strength and shield.

Pray for all men and women in our prisons, that though in the past they yielded to temptation, God's voice may be heard in their quiet cells.

Pray for all who for their own ends tempt others, that their eyes may be opened to the evil they do.

Lead us not into temptation, but deliver us from evil.

Grant, O God, that we may never run into those temptations which in our prayers we desire to avoid.*

SELF-DEDICATION

" For their sakes I sanctify Myself, that they also might be sanctified through the truth. . . . I am the good Shepherd: the good Shepherd giveth His life for the sheep. . . ."—John xvii. 19 ; x. 11.

" If any man would come after Me, let him deny himself, and take up his cross, and follow Me. —Matt. xvi. 24.

Other Readings : Matt. x. 37-39 ; Mark x. 17-22, 29-31 ; Luke xiv. 27-33 ; Eph. v. 1, 2 ; Phil. iii. 7-14 ; Heb. xi. 24-27.

A MEDITATION

Think how Jesus' life was one long act of self-giving ; at home in Nazareth ; throughout Galilee ; for the sick and wretched ; for His disciples ; and how at last He offered Himself in the prime of His strong manhood to suffer and die for the whole world.

> *All this Thou didst for me.*
> *What have I done for Thee ?*

Jesus asks us to deny ourselves, *not just special* things. *He wants us to be altogether His, in thought and will and act. He may sometimes require of us to give up things we would like to have or to do ; but an easy life, with no renunciation in it, is never the finest and strongest—or even the most joyful.*

THANKSGIVING

I thank Thee, O Heavenly Father—
> for Jesus Christ Who gave Himself for my sake ;
> that His Spirit still works on in men, giving them the joy of service ;
> for the sacrifices which mothers gladly make for their children ;

for the work of doctors and nurses, and of all
who lose themselves in the care of others ;
for the patience of those who endure wrong
quietly, and for the love which pays the
price of forgiveness for Christ's sake ;
for all those who in countless unknown acts
of love will manifest the Spirit of Christ this
very day.

Bless, O God, all these dedicated lives, and
through them bless the world.

CONFESSION AND DEDICATION

Let me make confession
of thinking more of self than of others ;
of shrinking from difficult or costly service ;
of serving sullenly, and forgetting the joy set
before me ;
of selfish use of money, and forgetting the
claims of Christ's work.

O Lord Jesus Christ, Who for our sake didst
undergo want and shame and pain, we confess most
humbly that we have refused to share the burden
of Thy Cross, that we have denied Thee rather
than face mockery, and have sought comfort and
security. Forgive our sins, help us to amend, and
give us courage to endure. Amen.*

Here, O Lord, we offer and present to Thee ourselves, souls and bodies, to be a reasonable, holy
and living sacrifice, humbly beseeching Thee that
Thou wilt accept this our offering, and use us for
the work of Thy Kingdom, and the making known
Thy love to all mankind. Through Jesus Christ
our Lord. Amen.

RECREATION

" I am come that they might have life, and that they might have it more abundantly."—John x. 10.

Other Readings : Psalm lxxxix. 14-18 ; Matt. v. 13-16 ; Luke xv. 11-32 ; John xv. 4-11 ; Rom. xiv. 7-9 ; Hymn 673 ; Hymn 647.

We all have times of leisure when we are free, more or less, to do as we please. How are we to make the very best of such times, so as to enter by them into that full life which Christ calls us to live ? Think over the following suggestions :

A Christian will use his leisure with purpose, with zest and with freedom, so that it will be a real recreation for work.

A Christian will want to feel that Christ is with him in every part of his life. That will help him to decide what he may, or may not, do with his leisure ; what pleasures he may take with unclouded freedom ; what amount of money he may spend on his pleasures without being luxurious or selfish.

A Christian will think out with special care how he will spend the leisure of Sunday, so that each week that day will stand out as a really fine day in the best sense.

A Prayer

All praise to Thee who safe hast kept,
And hast refreshed me while I slept. . . .
Guard my first springs of thought and will,
And with Thyself my spirit fill.

O God our Father, Who didst send Christ into the world that we might learn through Him the secret of life, I thank Thee for this new day, and for the interests and joys of living with Christ as Master and Friend.   For every happy hour I have known, for the satisfaction of doing good work, for all wholesome activities of body and mind, for friendships in which I have given and taken with freedom of heart, for beauty enjoyed, and for all clean mirth, I praise and bless Thee.   Especially to-day I thank Thee for hours of rest and recreation.

Forgive me, O Father, for any clouds that I have drawn upon my leisure hours through selfishness, through false ideas of freedom, or through narrow thoughts of Thy great Kingdom and Fatherly love.

Set in my heart a pure and steadfast love of all things fair and good and true.   Give me in all my pursuits, at work or at play, alone or with my friends, a sense of the blessing of Christ, the Prince of Life ; and help me so to use this day that I may come unstained and refreshed in body and spirit to the first day of the week, and give thanks to Him Who rose from the dead, and lives for ever.

> Direct, control, suggest, this day
> All I design, or do, or say,
> That all my powers, with all their might,
> To Thy sole glory may unite.
> Through Jesus Christ our Lord.   Amen.

INTERCESSION

Pray for the friends you will be with this afternoon . . .

> for children who have only the street to play in . . .
> for people tired out by their work, who must use their leisure for rest alone . . .
> for your minister in his preparation for to-morrow.

THE REDEMPTION OF THE WORLD

" And Jesus came to them and spake unto them, saying, All authority hath been given unto Me in heaven and on earth. Go ye therefore, and make disciples of all the nations, baptising them into the name of the Father and of the Son and of the Holy Spirit ; teaching them to observe all things whatsoever I commanded you : and lo, I am with you alway, even unto the end of the world." —Matt. xxviii. 18-20.

Other Readings : Isa. xlii. ; Acts xvi. 9-15 ; Acts xvii. 16-34 ; Acts xxvi. 15-23 ; Rom. x. 12-15 ; Rev. vii. 9-17 ; Hymn 372.

The world's greatest need is for Jesus Christ. Think of how we all sin and suffer because we will not let Christ fully into our lives, to show us how to live, to give us the love and power of God. Think of the world-wide suffering and fear and cruelty due to men's ignorance of what God is like. And Jesus is " the Way and the Truth and the Life." Think of the love of God, yearning over all His creatures in all the world through all the ages, and calling those who have begun to know Him to spread that knowledge and bring all the world to Him through the Gospel of Jesus.

O Heavenly Father, Who hast created all mankind to be Thy children, pour into my heart that love with which Thou hast loved the world. Make me to see the world's need of Thee, and to think with compassion of those who wander and suffer because they do not know the truth as it is in Jesus. Do Thou warm my cold heart with an imagination of Thy great purpose for the world, and with the remembrance of what Thy brave missionary servants have done in many lands for its redemption.

INTERCESSION

Now pray to God, with imagination and with expectancy, for—

all Christ's servants in the foreign mission field this very day . . . those who are preaching . . . or teaching . . . or helping to heal diseases . . ., especially any missionaries known to yourself . . .

all native Churches in non-Christian lands that especially need wisdom and stability . . .

the Church of Christ everywhere to-day . . . and all true servants of God's Kingdom every day . . . in the service of mankind.

SELF-DEDICATION

O Lord our God, I praise Thee for the living picture of Thyself that Thou hast given us in Jesus Christ. Forgive us that we have tried to accept Thy gift so selfishly, ministering to ourselves with narrow hearts when Thy love was yearning over all mankind.

O King of Love, Who hast called us to march under Thy banner, teach us, in great things or in small, as we have opportunity, to bear the burdens of the world, and with joy to deny ourselves for its redemption ; whether here at home, or in distant lands, according to Thy call ; through Jesus Christ our Lord. Amen.

March we forth in the strength of God, with the banner of Christ unfurled,
That the light of the glorious gospel of truth may shine throughout the world :
Fight we the fight with sorrow and sin, to set their captives free,
That the earth may be filled with the glory of God, as the waters cover the sea.

GETTING AND SPENDING

" Lay not up for yourselves treasures upon earth, where moth and rust doth corrupt, and where thieves break through and steal : but lay up for yourselves treasures in heaven, where neither moth nor rust doth corrupt, and where thieves do not break through nor steal ; for where your treasure is, there will your heart be also. . . . No man can serve two masters : for either he will hate the one, and love the other : or else he will hold to the one, and despise the other. . . . Ye cannot serve God and mammon."—Matt. vi. 19-21, 24.

" . . . Get your promised contribution ready in good time. I want it to be forthcoming as a generous gift, not as money wrung out of you. Mark this : he who sows sparingly will reap sparingly, and he who sows generously will reap a generous harvest. Everyone is to give what he has made up his mind to give ; there is to be no grudging or compulsion about it, for God loves the giver who gives cheerfully."—2 Cor. ix. 5-7. (Moffatt.)

Other Readings : Deut. viii. 10-18 ; Psalm lxii. 5-12 ; Matt. vi. 24-34 ; Luke xii. 13-21 ; 2 Cor. ix. 6-15 ; Phil. iv. 9-13.

Pause and think of God's generosity ; and of the spirit in which you should accept it : with deep gratitude ; and with the sense of a trust committed to you.

Fountain of good, to own Thy love
Our thankful hearts incline ;
What can we render, Lord, to Thee,
When all the worlds are Thine ?

SELF-EXAMINATION

Am I grateful for the things I have ? Do I envy those who are better off than I am ? Do I give
42

good value for my earnings ? Am I willing to share my possessions with others ? Would the loss of money take away my happiness ? Am I scrupulously honest in money matters ? Can I be satisfied before God with losing money, or with winning money, by gambling ? Do I spend too much on luxuries ? Do I do my best to keep out of debt ? Do I give as much as I ought to the work of the Church and to other good causes ?

Heavenly Father, cleanse my heart from all selfishness and unworthy ambition. Teach me to set store by the best things. Save me from meanness, and keep me from missing the way through the love of money and the things it buys. O Lord, make me faithful and diligent in my work, and honest in all my dealings with other people. Give me a grateful and generous heart. Make me quick to see the needs of others, and ready to help with more than sympathy.

Teach us, O Lord, that it is better to give than to receive ; better to forget ourselves than to put ourselves forward ; better to minister than to be ministered unto. And unto Thee, the God of Love, be glory and praise for ever. Amen.*

INTERCESSION

For those whose living is insecure ;
  for those who are in debt and see no way out of their troubles ;
  for those who make money dishonestly or by unworthy means ;
  for those who spend their money foolishly, and have no thought for the needs of others.

Give us, this day, our daily bread.

ETERNAL LIFE

" This is life eternal, that they should know Thee, the only true God, and Him whom Thou didst send, even Jesus Christ."—John xvii. 3.

" And I heard a great voice out of the throne saying, Behold, the tabernacle of God is with men, and He shall dwell with them, and they shall be His peoples, and God Himself shall be with them, and be their God : and He shall wipe away every tear from their eyes ; and death shall be no more ; neither shall there be mourning, nor crying, nor pain, any more : for the first things are passed away. And He that sitteth on the throne said, Behold I make all things new. . . . I am the Alpha and the Omega, the beginning and the end. I will give unto him that is athirst of the fountain of the water of life freely. He that overcometh shall inherit these things, and I will be his God, and he shall be My son."—Rev. xxi. 3-7.

Other Readings : Psalm xvi. 5-11 ; Jer. xxxi. 31-34 ; Isa. xxxv. ; Matt. vii. 24-27 ; Matt. xvi. 24-27 ; John xiv. 1-7.

" Eternal Life " does not just mean that when our bodies die our souls last on. It means a kind of life which we can begin to live here and now, and which cannot be destroyed by death, because it is united with God. In your office or shop or factory you may have on one side of you a man or woman who is living the merely temporal life, and on the other side, doing just the same work, another who is living the eternal. What will that eternal life be in its perfection ? You can find one imaginative picture of it in the above passage from Revelation, written by a man who had come to be very sure of it through Jesus Christ.

Eternal Father, I have lived too much for the things that do not last and do not count, and the end of a day has often brought me the sense of emptiness and failure.

    If I have lived more for self than for the great
        fellowship to which Thou callest me,
    if I have lived for appearance more than for
        truth,
            Forgive me.

Help me every day to see the glory of the things that are unseen and eternal : love and purity, truth and duty, courage and loyalty among my fellows, and the knowledge of Thee, O my God.

THANKSGIVING AND INTERCESSION

I praise Thee that Thou dost make me long for these things. I praise Thee that through Christ Thou hast revealed their deathless victory and the eternal life to which they lead. I praise Thee for all those dear to me who, having lived and died in the light of these eternal things, now live in Thee for ever.

May all my dear ones and friends so live in Thee. . . .

May those who have lost their friends by death be comforted by the light of Thine eternal life. . . .

(Let me pray for some whom I know.)

Eternal Father, teach us all to sink our little lives in Thy great life of love, with the spirit of Jesus Christ in our hearts. So may we be sharers in His victory, and in Thine eternity, and in the great fellowship of souls in all ages who have done Thy will and now see Thy face.

O God, Who hast prepared for them that love Thee such good things as pass man's understanding, pour into our hearts such love towards Thee that we, loving Thee above all things, may obtain Thy promises, which exceed all that we can desire ; through Jesus Christ our Lord. Amen.*

PRAYER

" O God, Thou art my God ; early will I seek
Thee : my soul thirsteth for Thee, my flesh longeth
for Thee in a dry and thirsty land, where no water
is ; to see Thy power and Thy glory, so as I have
seen Thee in the sanctuary. Because Thy loving-
kindness is better than life, my lips shall praise
Thee."—Psalm lxiii. 1-3.

" And when He had sent the multitudes away,
He came up into a mountain apart to pray : and
when the evening was come, He was there alone."
—Matt. xiv. 23.

Other Readings : Gen. xviii. 23-33 ; Matt. vi.
7-15 ; Matt. xxvi. 36-44 ; Mark i. 32-39 ; Luke
xi. 1-8 ; Luke xviii. 1-8.

*Prayer means coming to God, just as a child
comes to talk to his father because he loves him and
is lonely without him. We need to have time in our
prayers to think about God, to speak to Him of our
love, and to listen for His voice. Henry Drummond
said : " Ten minutes spent in Christ's society every
day, ay, two minutes, if it be face to face and
heart to heart, will make the whole life different."*

O God, my Father, I come to seek for Thee.
Thou hast made me for Thyself, and my heart is
restless until it rest in Thee. Help me to feel Thy
presence now, and to see Thy glory.

O Lamb of God, that takest away the sin of the
world, for Thy loneliness and failure, for Thy stress
of spirit and Thy strong prayer, for Thy Cross upon
the hill, for Thy death that giveth life, for Thy life
that overcometh death, we worship Thee our Lord
and Master, our Saviour and Redeemer.*

Jesus said :—

" Ask and the gift will be yours,
      seek and you will find,
46

knock and the door will open to you ;
for everyone who asks receives,
the seeker finds,
the door is opened to anyone who
knocks."

Matt. vii. 7, 8. (Moffatt.)

" If ye shall ask anything in My name, I will
do it."—John xiv. 14.

*As a child tells his father about the things he
wants, we may speak to God of our needs and desires
—whether for ourselves or for our friends or for the
world ; and Jesus assures us that such prayer has
great results. Only we must pray " in faith,
nothing wavering." And we must remember that
to pray in Christ's Name means to pray only for
the kind of things He would ask for if He were in
our place.*

Breathe on me, Breath of God,
Until my heart is pure,
Until with Thee I will one will
To do and to endure.

Lord, teach me to pray : and help me now to
pray . . . for the needs of my own life . . . for
forgiveness for my sins, for help against my temptations, for more love to Thee . . . (speak to God
about your other needs . . .) for my home, for
each member of the family . . . for Thy Kingdom
of purity and love, and for anything I may be able
to do to help it by my life to-day among my
fellows.

These things I ask in Christ's Name. Amen.

GOD AND MY FEARS

" God is our refuge and our strength,
    In straits a present aid ;
Therefore, although the earth remove,
    We will not be afraid."
                            Psalm xlvi. 1, 2.

" Be strong and of a good courage. . . . The
Lord, He it is that doth go before thee ; He will
be with thee, He will not fail thee, neither forsake thee : fear not, neither be dismayed."—Deut.
xxxi. 7-8.

" He that had received the one talent came and
said, Lord, I knew thee that thou art a hard man
. . . and I was afraid, and went away and hid
thy talent in the earth. . . . But his lord answered
and said unto him, Thou wicked and slothful
servant."—Matt. xxv. 24-26.

Other Readings : Exod. iii. 11-15 ; Psalm lxxiii.
21-26 ; Isa. xliii. 1, 2 ; Luke v. 4-11 ; Rom. viii. 14-
18 ; 1 John iv. 13-19.

    *You would not wish your life to be so hampered
by fears and worries that Jesus would call you a
" wicked and slothful servant."   Therefore resolve
to put them away as unworthy, remembering*
        that you belong to God ;
        that God knows all about your fears ;
        that God is your refuge ;
        that your part is only to trust.

If thou but suffer God to guide thee,
    And hope in Him through all thy ways,
He'll give thee strength, whate'er betide thee,
    And bear thee through the evil days ;
Who trusts in God's unchanging love
Builds on the rock that naught can move.

THANKSGIVING

O God, Who art my refuge and my strength, I thank Thee for all the words of hope and courage in the Bible,

> for the sense of Thy presence near me,

> for Thy knowledge of my weakness and my fears,

> and above all for Jesus Christ, victorious over fear and sin and death, and ever calling me to share His victory.

> Just as I am, young, strong and free,
> To be the best that I can be
> For truth, and righteousness, and Thee,
> Lord of my life, I come.

INTERCESSION

Hear me, O Lord, as I ask Thee to uphold with Thy strong spirit all those who are crippled by fears of any kind : all who shrink from the brave adventure of life, whose spirits are held in bondage by the fear of death, or darkened by the dread of ill-health or poverty ; all who are hampered by the fear of criticism ; all who amid their temptations distrust themselves and have not learned to trust in Thee. I ask Thy blessing on all men and women who are leading the great Christian enterprises : those who are thinking great thoughts, those who are doing great deeds, those who are suffering pain or loneliness or misunderstanding for Christ's sake, and who by their heroism are leading many timid souls to Thyself. Hear me for the sake of Jesus Christ, our Lord and Master. Amen.

PEACE

" Blessed are the meek : for they shall inherit the
      earth.
Blessed are they that hunger and thirst after
      righteousness : for they shall be filled.
Blessed are the merciful : for they shall obtain
      mercy.
Blessed are the pure in heart : for they shall see
      God.
Blessed are the peacemakers : for they shall be
      called sons of God."—Matt. v. 5-9.

" And when He drew nigh, He saw the city, and
wept over it, saying, If thou hadst known in this
day, even thou, the things which belong unto
peace ! but now they are hid from thine eyes."
—Luke xix. 41, 42.

Other Readings :   Psalm lxxii. 1-8 ;   Isa. ii. 2-5 ;
Zech. ix. 9-10 ;   Matt. v. 38-48 ;   Gal. v. 19-26 ;
Eph. ii. 13-18.

> *Let me very eagerly dedicate myself as a follower
> of Christ to the cause of peace on earth.   The vital
> matter is not simply to keep crying Peace, but to
> seek the things that make for peace, to get the hearts
> of men filled with the passion for righteousness,
> with the peace of God, with the love of mankind,
> with the spirit of Christ.*

O God, Who art Peace everlasting, Whose chosen
reward is the gift of peace, and Who hast taught
that the peacemakers are Thy children, pour Thy
peace into our souls, that all discord may utterly
vanish, and all that makes for peace be sweet to
us for ever ; through Jesus Christ our Lord.*

I praise Thee, O God of Peace, for Jesus Christ
Thy Son, Who breaks down the barriers between
God and man, and between man and man ;

for all the men and women who through the ages have worked for His sake to bring peace;
for every act of kindness and understanding in home, in business, or among my friends, that has brought goodwill.

Forgive us, O God, one and all, for the wrongs that have delayed the day of peace.
We have so failed to follow Christ that—
in our homes there has been selfishness and strife ;
in our daily work there has been discontent, suspicion and self-seeking ;
as a nation we have aimed at our own glory and wealth, and have forgotten that we are called to serve the peoples of the world.

INTERCESSION

Pour out, O Father, upon our nation, and upon all the world, the spirit of brotherhood. May those who profess the name of Christ be more willing to take His way, and to trust it, in the great affairs of the world. May rich and poor, employers and employed, be drawn together in mutual service, and so may the world's industry be blessed with peace. Lead Thou the nations, with their varied gifts and traditions, into understanding and friendship, that wars may be no more, but peace prevail in all the world.
Bless the work of the Church for world-friendship. . . .
Bless the League of Nations. . . .

Forgive me, O Heavenly Father, for every root of bitterness in my own heart, and pluck it out. Help me daily to live with Thy peace and love in my heart, and to work and pray for the coming of Thy Kingdom of universal brotherhood.
Through Jesus Christ, Thy Son, Our Elder Brother. Amen.

MY BODY

" Know ye not that your body is a temple of the Holy Spirit which is in you, which ye have from God ? and ye are not your own ; for ye were bought with a price : glorify God therefore in your body."—1 Cor. vi. 19, 20.

" I beseech you therefore, brethren, by the mercies of God, to present your bodies a living sacrifice, holy, acceptable to God, which is your reasonable service."—Rom. xii. 1.

Other Readings : Psalm xxiv. ; Psalm cxxi. ; Matt. xviii. 7-9 ; Matt. xxvi. 26-28 ; 1 Cor. ix. 24-27 ; James iii. 1-18.

Let your mind dwell on Jesus in the days of His flesh : how full of vitality and power He was ; how He worked at the carpenter's bench in Nazareth ; how He toiled and how He rested in the years of His public ministry ; His crowded hours of work, His quiet vigils. Think how much time He gave to the healing of the sick. Think of how He spoke at the end about His own body, which He was going to give on the Cross. Can you doubt that God, Who gave Christ as the pattern of manhood, means you to keep your body, as well as your soul, fit and keen in His service ?

THANKSGIVING AND INTERCESSION

Lord of my life, Who hast created my body to be the temple of Thy Holy Spirit, I give Thee thanks for those bodily gifts which can be made to serve that end : for the sight of the eyes, the hearing of the ears, the power of speech, the strength of the arm, the precious gift of health ; for fresh air to breathe, and all the delight of wholesome exercise and recreation.

Remember, O God, and teach me always to remember, those who are debarred by ill-health, or by circumstance, from the joys of bodily activity.

Be kind, O God, and make me kind, to the blind, the deaf, the dumb.

Let Thy kind eye be upon all of us who to-day will be seeking fresh air and exercise. May Thy blessing be upon us in this, O Thou Whose delights are with the sons of men.

PENITENCE AND RESOLUTION

Are you slack about the besetting sins connected with your body? Sins of appetite and gluttony; laziness; vanity in dress; unclean imagination, or impure trifling with God-created instincts. Remember that such sins can only be overcome if we start the right sort of habits all round—in the friendships we make, in the books we read, in the pictures we look at, in our thoughts and desires; and above all by getting into our lives noble interests, divine enthusiasms.

O my God, Who hast given me a body to keep pure and clean and healthy for Thy service, forgive me for all my failure and unfaithfulness in this great charge. Forgive me for every mean use which I have made of Thy gifts, in thought or word or deed.

Create in me a clean heart, O God, and give me a steadfast will. Help me to know myself, to reverence myself, and so to manage myself that, clean and wholesome in heart and life, I may be a strength to others around me in keeping straight and pure. Teach me to reverence my body and the bodies of my fellow-creatures. Help me to see the glory of perfect manhood in Jesus Christ. Make me to be so captivated by the things for which He lived and died that all my passions and energies will be caught up into the enthusiasm of His service, and evil things will lose their power. O my God, Who canst make of me what Thou wouldst have me be, I would offer myself unto Thee, without fear or brooding, body and soul. May my body be the servant of my spirit, and both body and spirit be servants of Thine. Through Jesus Christ. Amen.

WORSHIP

" And Moses said, I will now turn aside, and see this great sight, why the bush is not burnt. And when the Lord saw that he turned aside to see, God called unto him out of the midst of the bush, and said, Moses, Moses. And he said, Here am I. And He said, Draw not nigh hither : put off thy shoes from off thy feet, for the place whereon thou standest is holy ground."—Exod. iii. 3-5.

" I was in the Spirit on the Lord's day, and heard behind me a great voice, as of a trumpet. . . . And I turned to see the voice that spake with me. . . . And when I saw Him, I fell at His feet as dead. And He laid His right hand upon me, saying unto me, Fear not ; I am the first and the last ; I am He that liveth, and was dead ; and behold I am alive for evermore."—Rev. i. 10, 12, 17, 18.

Other Readings : 2 Chron. vi. 1-21 ; Psalm xcvi. ; Psalm cxxii. ; Luke iv. 16-22 ; Luke xxiv. 13-32 ; Acts ii. 14-28.

Withdraw your thoughts from everything else, and direct them quietly towards God, Whom you will to-day be worshipping through Jesus Christ : God, the All-Great . . . the All-Holy . . . the All-Loving. . . .

My God, how wonderful Thou art,
  Thy majesty how bright!
How beautiful Thy mercy-seat,
  In depths of burning light !

O how I fear Thee, living God,
  With deepest, tenderest fears ;
And worship Thee with trembling hope,
  And penitential tears !

Yet I may love Thee too, O Lord,
  Almighty as Thou art,
For Thou hast stooped to ask of me
  The love of my poor heart.

Think of what Sunday should mean to Christians. It is above all else the day on which, every week, we remember the rising of Jesus Christ from the dead, and meet together in His Name for reverent and joyful worship.

Father in Heaven, Who, as on this glad day, didst raise from the dead our Lord Jesus Christ, I thank Thee for the new hope and joy and power that came into the world through His resurrection. I thank Thee that to-day in every land His followers are meeting together to worship Thee. I thank Thee for every memory I have of Thy presence and Thy love made plain to me in Thy House. Help me to-day to come before Thee with such a humble and loving heart that I may find Thee and be found by Thee.

Forgive me, O Father, for all my unfaithfulness to Thee in daily life. May my fellowship to-day with Thee and with Thy people lift me above my failures, and strengthen me for nobler living through the common days of this week.
Hear me now as I pray for—
    my minister. . . .
    my fellow-worshippers. . . .
May all Thy worshippers this day, here and in all the world, approach Thy House with thoughts of prayer to Thee and of love to one another. Hallowed be Thy Name, this day.

Grant us, O Lord, to pass through this day in gladness and peace, without stumbling and without stain ; that, reaching the eventide victorious over all temptation, we may praise Thee, the Eternal God, Who art blessed, and dost govern all things, world without end.   Amen.*

OUR DAILY WORK

" Ye call Me Master and Lord : and ye say well ;
for so I am.   If I then, your Lord and Master, have
washed your feet : ye also ought to wash one
another's feet.   For I have given you an example,
that ye should do as I have done to you.   Verily,
verily, I say unto you, The servant is not greater
than his lord ; neither he that is sent greater than
he that sent him.   If ye know these things, happy
are ye if ye do them."—John xiii. 13-17.

" Not in the way of eye-service, as men-pleasers ;
but as servants of Christ, doing the will of God from
the heart ; with goodwill doing service, as unto
the Lord, and not unto men."—Eph. vi. 6, 7.

Other Readings : Exod. xxxv. 30-35 ; Eccles. xi.
1-6 ; Luke xvi. 10-13 ; Acts xx. 33-35 ; Phil. ii.
4-8 ; 2 Thess. iii. 6-13.

THANKSGIVING AND DEDICATION

Almighty God, our Maker and our Father, Whose
works all praise Thee, I worship and adore Thee in
Thy ceaseless work of creating and providing for
the needs of all mankind. Especially I would
adore Thee for Thy greatest gift to men, Jesus
Christ, Thy Son, our Lord. I praise Thee that He
was born in poverty, that He lived in a workman's
home, that He knew want and weariness, and
shared in the humblest toil. I thank Thee that
He is willing to enter into every part of my life,
and to make my daily work great by saying, " Ye
have done it unto Me."

Thank God for your daily work and for strength
to do it.   Offer your daily work to God, asking His
pardon for discontent . . . a grudging spirit . . .
indolence . . . badly done work.

Teach me, O Lord, the way of patient industry, that in all the work my hands find to do I may honour and praise Thee. Make me to know the true dignity of all honest work, and keep me faithful in small and humble tasks. Enable me to work as a good comrade with all my fellow-workers, and make me brave to fight against all conditions of work that hurt or hinder fulness of life.

INTERCESSION

Father of all, I give Thee thanks for the great world of men and women at work ; for the courage, faithfulness and skill that go into their daily toil, and that make possible the comforts and privileges I enjoy.

I ask Thy help for—
    all who labour and are heavy laden to-day ;
    all whose toil is without hope and without
        honour ;
    all who are over-worked and underpaid, men
        and women out of work, and those dependent
        on them.

Heavenly Father, save us from all selfishness and thoughtlessness that would make the lot of others harder ; and teach those who love Thy Son to work and pray for the day when there will be leisure and health and honourable work for all. Let Thy work appear unto Thy servants and Thy glory unto their children. And let the beauty of the Lord our God be upon us ; and establish Thou the work of our hands upon us ; yea, the work of our hands, establish Thou it.

Through Jesus Christ our Lord. Amen.

FAITH

" If Thou canst do anything, have compassion on us and help us. And Jesus said unto him, If thou canst ! all things are possible to him that believeth. Straightway the father of the child cried out, and said, I believe; help Thou mine unbelief."—Mark ix. 22-24.

" Now faith means we are confident of what we hope for, convinced of what we do not see. It was for this that the men of old won their record. . . . Therefore, with all this host of witnesses encircling us, we must strip off every handicap, strip off sin with its clinging folds, to run our appointed course steadily, our eyes fixed upon Jesus as the pioneer and the perfection of faith."—Heb. xi. 1, 2, xii. 1, 2. (Moffatt.)

Other Readings : Matt. viii. 5-10 ; Matt. xv. 21-28 ; Mark v. 25-34 ; Luke xvii. 5, 6 ; Rom. v. 1-5 ; Heb. xi. 8-16, 32-40.

THANKSGIVING

My God and King, I praise Thee for all brave men and women who have believed in Thee, and by their faith have lived victorious lives. Especially I praise Thee for Jesus Christ ;

for the faith by which He conquered evil and endured the Cross, making it easier for all men to believe and trust in Thee, our God and Father;

for His calling of us to a stronger faith ;

for His showing us what faith can do in the world.

As you ask God to strengthen your faith, remember how much it depends on yourself and your own willingness to follow bravely the light God gives. Observe how Jesus used to reproach people

*for not having more faith. Remember that the
secret is to look away from yourself to God, as He
comes to you in Christ, and to commit yourself com-
pletely to Him. Take time now to do this, quietly
realising how near God is to you.*

Heavenly Father, I confess that I have not
trusted Thee as I ought. If I have been taking my
own way, lacking the faith and courage to take
Thine ; if I have not ventured enough for Thee ;
if I have been afraid to believe, day by day, in Thy
wonderful love and power, forgive me, O Heavenly
Father.

Lord, I believe : Help Thou my unbelief. In
times of perplexity keep me ever true to duty.
And make the light of the knowledge of Thy glory
to shine for me this day on the face of Jesus Christ.

INTERCESSION

Heavenly Father, I would ask these Thy best
blessings, not for myself alone, but for all that are
dear to me . . . ; for all who suffer pain or weakness, that they may be able to lay hold of Thy
strength and peace . . . for all who find faith
difficult through misfortune, injustice, bereave-
ment . . . for those who cannot trust Thee,
because they have not known the name of
Christ. . . .

O Lord, perfect, we beseech Thee, the faith of
us who believe, and sow the good seed of faith in
their hearts who as yet lack it ; that we all may
look steadfastly unto Thee, and run with patience
the race that is set before us. Give us grace to
show our faith by our works ; teach us to walk by
faith, having respect unto Thy promises ; which
of Thy mercy make good unto us in Thine own
good time, O our most gracious Lord God and
Saviour. Amen.*

SOLITUDE

" And in the morning, rising up a great while before day, He went out, and departed into a solitary place, and there prayed."—Mark i. 35.

" Behold, I stand at the door and knock : if any man hear My voice and open the door, I will come in to him, and will sup with him and he with Me." —Rev. iii. 20.

" Search me, O God, and know my heart : try me and know my thoughts : and see if there be any wicked way in me, and lead me in the way everlasting."—Psalm cxxxix. 23, 24.

Other Readings : Gen. xxxii. 24-31 ; Psalm cxxxix. 1-12 ; Psalm cxlii. ; Matt. vi. 5, 6 ; John xvi. 31-33 ; 2 Tim. iv. 16-18.

Consider how many things, both good and evil, have their roots in solitude. Every worst thing in my life has its roots in those times when I have shut myself up alone, away from my fellows and from God ; dallied with evil in imagination ; been slack, self-indulgent and self-pitiful in the hidden places of the heart. Every best thing in my life has its roots in those times when I have been alone with God ; listened for and heard His voice and direction ; been delivered by Him from the fear of man's blame and the love of man's praise ; fixed my mind on what is fine and big and worth while. " A man is what he is in the dark." " Thy presence makes the darkness light."

A PRAYER

I thank Thee, O Father, that Thou hast called me by Christ into communion with Thyself. Lift me now above all distracting and restless thoughts. Help me to be quiet in Thy presence, and let me taste and see that Thou art good.

A CONFESSION

O God, Thou knowest all my failure. I have not put Thee first in my thinking. In my inmost heart I have made room for evil thoughts, selfish desires, unkind criticisms, bitter grudges, secret envies. And these have borne their fruits in un-Christlike words and deeds, or in a mere show of goodness. O Spirit of Truth and Love, enter now my heart to cleanse and renew it.

PRAYERS

O Christ, be Thou my Comrade on this day's journey, that in my weakness Thy strength may be made perfect. Teach me to lean upon Thee from hour to hour, and help me to persevere in these resolves I now make in Thy sight. . . .

O God, Who settest the solitary in families, help me this day to be a loyal and hearty comrade to all my fellow-travellers, to respect them as Thy children, and to enter as a brother into all their joys and sorrows. Hear my prayer for all who must be alone, the aged, the sick, the friendless ; and especially for. . . .

> Teach us to look, in all our ends,
> On Thee for Judge, and not our friends ;
> That we, with Thee, may walk uncowed
> By fear or favour of the crowd.
> Through Christ our Lord. Amen.

MY RESPONSIBILITY

" Ye are the light of the world. . . . Let your light so shine before men, that they may see your good works, and glorify your Father Which is in heaven."—Matt. v. 14, 16.

Other Readings : Gen. iv. 8-10; Isa. lviii. 6-11; Ezek. xxxiii. 1-9; Luke xii. 41-48; Rom. xiv. 13-21; 1 Pet. ii. 9-12.

Father, Whose love within my heart leads me to pray to Thee, help me to come to a fuller understanding of Thy love. Help me to understand what Thy Fatherhood would mean to me if I had but the spirit of a child of Thine.

I confess that I have not lived as Thy child; that I have often failed to do Thy will; that by my selfishness and cowardice in daily life I have often denied Thee, making it harder for others to know Thee. For these my sins forgive me, O Father; and enable me to walk among men as a disciple of Jesus Christ, showing Him forth in word and deed.

Let me think of the claims of others, in a spirit of loyal burden-bearing.

" Then shall the righteous answer Him, saying, Lord, when saw we Thee an hungred and fed Thee ? or thirsty, and gave Thee drink ? When saw we Thee a stranger, and took Thee in ? or naked and clothed Thee. Or when saw we Thee sick, or in prison, and came unto Thee ? And the King shall answer and say unto them, Verily I say unto you, Inasmuch as ye have done it unto one of the least of these My brethren, ye have done it unto Me." —Matt. xxv. 37-40.

O Father, through whom all mankind on earth is bound together in brotherhood, help me, I pray

Thee, to realise and accept my responsibility towards others. . . .

Let me pray for my parents . . . my brothers and sisters . . . my companions at work or in recreation. Let me remember all that I owe to them, and thank God for the happiness that has come through them. . . .

Let me remember those on whose hard toil my comfort depends ; those who are poor and wretched ; those who have never sufficient food or clothing ; those who do not know the comfort of a clean, warm bed ; those who are out of work ; all the weak and unfortunate who have fallen into sin and forgotten God's love.

O heavenly Father, show me how I can help any such whom I know, and how I can so live my life as to be of service to those who need my help.

> O strengthen me, that, while I stand
> Firm on the rock, and strong in Thee,
> I may stretch out a loving hand
> To wrestlers with the troubled sea.

I would remember also the men and women of other countries. Help me to realise that they also are Thy children, O heavenly Father, and to give loyal help to every enterprise for their good. (Pray for Foreign Missions, pray for World Friendship.)

O Lord, give us grace, we beseech Thee, to hear and obey Thy voice which saith to every one of us, " This is the way, walk ye in it." Nevertheless, let us not hear it behind us saying, This is the way ; but rather before us saying, Follow Me. When Thou puttest us forth, go before us ; when the way is too great for us, carry us ; in the darkness of death, comfort us ; in the day of resurrection, satisfy us. Amen.*

THE KINGDOM OF GOD

" The kingdom of heaven is like unto leaven, which a woman took, and hid in three measures of meal, till the whole was leavened.

"Again the kingdom of heaven is like unto treasure hid in a field; the which when a man hath found, he hideth, and for joy thereof goeth and selleth all that he hath, and buyeth that field,

"Again, the kingdom of heaven is like unto a merchant man, seeking goodly pearls; who when he had found one pearl of great price, went and sold all that he had, and bought it."—Matt. xiii. 33, 44-46.

Other Readings : Psalm cxlv. 8-18 ; Isa. xi. 1-9 ; Luke x. 17-24 ; Luke xiii. 23-30 ; Luke xiv. 15-27 ; Luke xvii. 20-25.

The message of Jesus is the Gospel—the good news of the Kingdom of God. " The kingdom of God is at hand," said Jesus. " It is among you " —it is the greatest reality of life. God is always with us : we need pure hearts to see Him. Only if we are simple-minded enough, like little children believing in their father's goodness and trying to do his will, can we enter into the mystery of His Kingdom.

Almighty and everlasting God, Who didst send Thy Son Jesus Christ to tell us the good news of Thy Kingdom, Thou art the King of kings and Lord of lords. Thy Kingdom ruleth over all. O Thou who through all my life hast been seeking me, near unto me even when I have not known Thee or understood Thy love, help me to be sure of Thy presence now with me, and to be glad because of Thee.

Jesus said, " Blessed are the poor in spirit : for theirs is the kingdom of heaven."

O our Father, help us to be humble, setting far away from us all pride in our own wisdom and achievements, that day by day we may learn to walk with Thee as little children, understanding that Thy purpose is to rule in our hearts and lives by Thy love. Where we are blind to Thy presence, open our eyes. Purify our hearts that we may see Thee. Let Thy presence be dearer to us than all else, that we may be willing to give up whatever would hide it from us ; for the sake of Jesus Christ, Who brings Thee near to us. Amen.

Jesus taught us to pray : " Thy kingdom come : Thy will be done on earth as it is in heaven."

Almighty God, let Thy Kingdom come in my life. Be Thou the King of my heart. Rule Thou in my thoughts and affections ; in my work ; in my home-life and my friendships ; in my relations with other people ; in my recreations ; in the spending of my money ; in my prayers.

Thy Kingdom come everywhere :

In the turning of men and women in all the world to Thee ; through the work of the Church in this and all other lands ; through the faithful service and silent influence of men and women who love Thee ; in the healing of sickness ; in the writing of good books and clean newspapers ; in honest speech and straight dealing ; in the spread of peace.

> Thy Kingdom come, O God ;
>   Thy rule, O Christ, begin ;
> Break with Thine iron rod
>   The tyrannies of sin.
> O'er heathen lands afar
>   Thick darkness broodeth yet ;
> Arise, O Morning Star,
>   Arise and never set.

MY FRIENDSHIPS

" This is My commandment, that ye love one another, as I have loved you. Greater love hath no man than this, that a man lay down his life for his friends. Ye are My friends, if ye do whatsoever I command you. Henceforth I call you not servants ; for the servant knoweth not what his lord doeth ; but I have called you friends ; for all things that I have heard of My Father I have made known unto you."—John xv. 12-15.

Other Readings: 1 Sam. xviii. 1-4 ; 1 Sam. xix. 1-7 ; Luke x. 38-42 ; John i. 35-51 ; John xvii. 18-26 ; Phil. ii. 19-28 ; 2 Tim. i. 15-18.

Think of the friendship of Jesus. Its service— " *He began to wash the disciples' feet.*" *Its sympathy—*" *Jesus wept.*" *Its prayerfulness—* " *I have prayed for thee, that thy faith fail not.*" *Its attractiveness—*" *They came and told Jesus all they had done.*" *Its self-sacrifice—*" *He gave Himself for us.*" *Its joy—*" *The seventy returned again with joy. . . . In that hour Jesus rejoiced in spirit.*"

Thanksgiving

Lord, I humbly rejoice that Thou art willing to be my Friend. Help me now in the silence of my heart to feel Thy presence and to be glad in it.

For Thy love that came to find me and make me Thy friend, I thank Thee, O Lord.

For Thy trust in me even when I have failed Thee again and again, I thank Thee, O Lord.

For the knowledge that Thy friendship will make me more like Thee, until the day when I shall see Thee as Thou art, I thank Thee, O Lord.

Self-Examination

Do I share the greatest things in my life with my friends ? Or have I, through selfishness or fear of giving myself away, made it more difficult for them to believe in the friendship of Jesus ? Do I pray for them ?

Am I narrow in my friendships, withholding my love and interest from any except the one or two whom I find it easiest to like ?

O Thou Who art the Friend of all, and didst give Thyself to the uttermost for Thy friends, help me to see the best in everyone and to give my friendship bravely and joyfully in Thy strength. Amen.

INTERCESSION

I would now in silence pray for . . . and . . .

I would pray for all lonely people, who find it difficult to make friends, that we may not leave them out in the cold, but bring them into our fellowship.

I would pray for all missionaries, who by their life of friendship make Christ's friendship real to ignorant and despised peoples.

O Lord, grant us to love Thee with all our heart, and with all our mind, and with all our soul, and our neighbour for Thy sake, that the grace of charity and brotherly love may dwell in us, and all envy, harshness and ill-will may die in us. And fill our hearts with feelings of love, kindness and compassion, so that by constantly rejoicing in the happiness and good success of others, by sympathising with them in their sorrows, and putting away all harsh judgments and envious thoughts, we may follow Thee, Who art Thyself the true and perfect Love. Amen.*

BEFORE COMMUNION

Read Luke xxii. 14-32 ; 1 Cor. xi. 23-29.

Lord God Almighty, Thou Father, Saviour, and Comforter of souls : I thank Thee for Jesus Christ Thy Son, for His infinite love to all men, and for the sacraments which Thou hast given to be the signs of that love. To-day Thou art calling me to the Holy Table of Remembrance. I feel myself unworthy to draw nigh, for I am poor in everything Thou desirest to see in me—in faith and goodness, in loyalty and love. I confess that I have been content with standards lower than Christ sets for me. I have been careless of His claims, and eager in the pursuit of my own pleasure and advantage. I have been self-satisfied and self-indulgent, and while ready to condemn the faults of others, I have not been slow to excuse my own. For these and all my sins help me truly to repent, and to believe in Thy forgiving mercy, through Jesus Christ my Lord.

Cleanse now the thoughts and desires of my heart, by Thy Holy Spirit, that with lowly faith I may venture to Thy Table. Open my eyes to see Him who waits there to be gracious. As through the symbols of His broken body and shed blood I see Him dying upon the Cross, help me by faith and love to receive Him into my heart. And help me to see Him in His risen life and power, in the midst of His people according to His promise, living and loving as at the first.

Father of Jesus, Lord of my life, help me and all my fellow-worshippers this day so to feel the power of His love that with sincere hearts we may renew our vows as His disciples and soldiers ; and as He gave all for us and kept nothing back, enable us henceforward to live not for ourselves but for Him who loved us and gave Himself for us. These things I ask for His Name's sake. Amen.

AFTER COMMUNION

Heavenly Father, I praise and thank Thee for Thy goodness to me this day, and especially for calling me to Thy Table to commemorate the love and sacrifice of Thy dear Son, my Lord. I bless Thee for all Thou hast enabled me to see of the meaning of His Cross and of the power of His love to save, for communion with Him in His risen life, and for the wonderful gifts of grace bestowed by Him upon me.

Let the memory of all I have seen and received be a guard and defence to me, a shield against temptation, a wall against evil. Let the Spirit that was in Jesus dwell in me also, that I may be humble as He was humble, loving as He was loving, unselfish and diligent as He was in serving others and doing Thy holy will. Thou who desirest truth in the inward parts, give me sincerity. Thou from whom nothing is hid, save me from falseness or unfaithfulness in thought or word or deed. Enable me to break with every unworthy habit that would hold me back from following Christ, and to give up every indulgence that would weaken my power to serve Him. Thou that callest me to self-surrender, help me to obey and hold nothing back.

Give me a greater desire to pray, and a deeper joy in Thy worship. Be Thou the Companion of all my way, saving me by Thy presence. If danger come, give me courage; if hardship, endurance; if temptation, strength to be faithful, cost what it may. If my faith grow faint, revive it; if my hope burn low, rekindle it; if my feet slip, hold me up. Grant me always to fight the good fight of faith, to win the victory, and at last to receive the crown, through Jesus Christ my Lord. Amen.

CHRISTMAS

" Unto you is born this day in the city of David a Saviour which is Christ the Lord."

" Though Christ a thousand times
In Bethlehem be born,
If He's not born in thee,
Thy soul's forlorn."

Heavenly Father, I thank Thee for the remembrance this day of Him Who was born to be the Saviour of the world. I thank Thee that He was once a little child, depending on human love and care, and that through Him Thou dost come very near to us Thy children. I pray that Christ may be born in my heart to-day ; and that through His life in me I may have that childlike spirit which He loved to bless. Keep me, O God, from thinking of myself too much. Help me to obey Thee and to trust Thee with a simple heart. Keep me pure and kind through the happiness of this Christmastide.

Intercession

I pray Thee to bless all little children to-day : the children whom I specially love, that they may be true children of Thine ; all children that are unloved and neglected, that Thou wilt send them helpers and friends ; children born in heathen lands, that they may come to learn of Thy Holy Child Jesus.

(Ask yourself whether you know of any little child to whom you can bring some happiness to-day for Christ's sake.)

Heavenly Father, let the spirit of the Prince of Peace win all the world, that wars may cease and men may live together as Thy children. And help us all to make more room for Christ in our common days, that His peace may fill our hearts and lives. This we ask in His Name. Amen.

NEW YEAR'S DAY

Read Psalm xc. ; or Mark i. 16-20 ; or Hymn 601 ;
or Hymn 606.

I thank Thee that to those who love Thee
The best is ever yet to be :
That, if we abide in Thee, we can never grow old,
For Thou, our Master, art eternally young,
Eternally radiant with the joyful energy, the fresh-
    ness and buoyancy of youth.*

God of my life, Who hast brought me to the
beginning of a new year, I thank Thee for Thy
goodness to me all the days and years of my life,
and especially for all the gifts of Thy love in the
year that has ended. (Stop and think gratefully
of some of them. . . .)
Forgive me for my wasted days and hours, and
my forgotten resolves. Help me to accept this
new year from Thy hand with joy and zest, with
faith, hope and love. For all its duties and
experiences give me courage and wisdom. Save
me from being discouraged by my failures, keep
me from being unworthily content, teach me to
expect great things from Thee in the high service
to which Thou callest me. As the years pass may
I come to know Thee better and follow Jesus Christ
more faithfully.

Heavenly Father, bless Thou this day, and
through all this year, those who are dear to me,
the folk in my home, and my friends. . . .
Give some portion of hope and joy to all who at
this season feel their loneliness ; those who have
no family or friends around them for good fellowship ; those who are far from home. Help us to
be kind to those who most need our kindness.
Keep us unselfish through all our pilgrimage. And
bring us finally, by Thy mercy, to our eternal
home.
Through Jesus Christ, the same yesterday, to-day
and for ever. Amen.

GOOD FRIDAY

" And when they were come to the place which is called Calvary, there they crucified Him and the malefactors, one on the right hand and the other on the left. Then said Jesus, Father, forgive them; for they know not what they do. And they parted His raiment, and cast lots. And the people stood beholding."—Luke xxiii. 33-35.

O love of God! O sin of man!
In this dread act your strength is tried,
And victory remains with love:
Jesus, our Lord, is crucified!

The death of Jesus on the Cross speaks in the language of deeds what words cannot express. It shows us sin working itself out—not extraordinary sins, but the common sins of jealousy, selfishness, narrow-minded religious prejudice, cowardice, with which we are all acquainted. In the same way, it is the pledge of God's love to us: it shows us how far Divine Love can go for sinful men.

Let us pray that—
    as Christ bore His Cross, with its shame and sorrow, we may bravely endure trials, sufferings and mockery when they come;
    as Christ asked forgiveness for those who crucified Him, we may be able to love and forgive those who hurt or injure us;
    as Christ in His love was crucified by human sin, we may learn from His Cross to hate evil and to believe in the love of God.

O God, my Father, who in the Cross of Thy dear Son, hast made known to all the world the vastness of Thy love, help me to hate all the sins that crucify Christ afresh in the world to-day. Give me the spirit of Christ that I may never prefer comfort before duty, or shrink from the way of sacrifice and suffering because it is too hard. In all things may I be willing to take up my cross and follow Him. Amen.

EASTER DAY

" Fear not ye : for I know that ye seek Jesus,
Which was crucified. He is not here ; for He is
risen."—Matt. xxviii. 5, 6.

> Ye children of the light,
>   Arise with Him, arise ;
> See how the Daystar bright
>   Is burning in the skies !
> Leave in the grave beneath
>   The old things passed away ;
> Buried with Him in death,
>   O live with Him to-day.

All-glorious Father of spirits, Who dwellest in
eternity, in wonder and rejoicing I lift my heart
to Thee, who hast planted in me the faith and hope
that look beyond the grave.   Let Christ's risen life
dwell in me this day, that I may rise with Him
above all that wars against my soul, into clean
thoughts, holy affections, and power to serve Thee
with freedom and joy.   Help me to purify myself
even as He was pure, to deny every evil inclination,
and to live the life of goodness, truth and love.
Keep high within me the faith by which I may
overcome the world.   Give me a firm assurance
that nothing now can separate me from Thy love,
and that over all dark and hostile things I may
be more than conqueror, through Jesus Christ my
Lord.

Grant, I beseech Thee, O God, that wherever His
disciples may gather this day He may be in the
midst of them, and say, " Peace be unto you,"
and breathe on them His Spirit.   And wherever
any are sad and downcast let Him draw near to
them, to open to them the Scriptures and turn their
sorrow into joy.

73

WHITSUNDAY

" Ye shall receive power, after that the Holy Spirit is come upon you : and ye shall be witnesses unto Me."—Acts i. 8.

Other Readings : John xiv. 25-27 ; John xvi. 7-15 ; Acts ii. 1-21 ; 1 Cor. xii. 4-11.

O God my Father, I have seen Thy glory and Thy love on the face of Jesus Christ. I have longed to know Thee and to obey Thee, to make of my life something worthy of Thy love. But I have failed. Thou knowest how often I have been disloyal to Thee, how I have yielded myself to chance desires and passing interests, and not to Thy will. Thou knowest how poor I am in the knowledge and love of Thee. Thou knowest how little I have followed Jesus Christ Thy Son. I am ashamed, O God, to call myself Thy servant or His disciple.

Show me, O my God, this day, the great things Thou hast done and canst still do for Thy children. Thou didst come in great power upon Thy Church at Pentecost ; Thou didst move weak men by Thy Spirit, and they went out in joy and power to change the world. Thou hast in all ages entered the hearts of Thy saints, lifting them above fear and selfishness, until men saw in them the love and power of Christ. I praise Thee, O God, for the remembrance of it this day, and for the assurance that Thou, our Heavenly Father, wilt still give Thy Holy Spirit to those who ask Thee.

O Holy Spirit of Truth and Love, come Thou and dwell in my heart. Help me to yield my life to Thee. May I live day by day in a power that is not my own, and a joy no man can take from me. Help me, and all my fellow-worshippers, and Thy Church in all the world, to worship Thee this day in spirit and in truth, with joy and gladness, and every day to be witnesses in the world to Jesus Christ our Lord and Master. Amen.

ON LEAVING HOME

"And Jacob went out from Beersheba, and went toward Haran. And he lighted upon a certain place, and tarried there all night, because the sun was set; and he took one of the stones of the place and put it under his head, and lay down in that place to sleep. And he dreamed, and behold a ladder set up on the earth, and the top of it reached to heaven: and behold the angels of God ascending and descending on it. . . . And Jacob awaked out of his sleep, and he said, Surely the Lord is in this place; and I knew it not."—Gen. xxviii. 10-12, 16.

Other Readings: Paraphr. ii.; Rom. viii. 35-39; Ezek. xi. 16.

Gracious Father, I praise Thee that Thou art the Guide of my life. Help me now to feel Thee near, to know that Thou wilt never leave me nor forsake me.

Remember that when you leave home and friends, and go among strangers, you still belong to Christ. You must try to be worthy of His Name in your daily life. And remember that, wherever you find His Church, it is there waiting for you—to help you and to be helped by you. Now commit yourself in faith and obedience to God.

Now, O Father, grant that Thy presence may go with me and be a home to me wherever I may dwell. Make me to know the safety of Thy love, and the shelter of Thy power. May Thy Spirit keep me from the things that would grieve Thee, or bring shame to those who love me. Bless all who are dear to me. Comfort them with Thy presence. May they ever know the warmth and gladness of Thy love; and though distance separates us help us to feel near to one another, because we are all near to Thee. And whatever of change the future may bring, keep us faithful to Thee, Our Father, and to the one Eternal Home, where partings are no more. Amen.

THE SHADOW OF DEATH

Readings: Psalm xxiii.; Psalm ciii.; Rom. viii. 31-39 ; 1 Cor. xv. 53-57 ; 1 Pet. i. 3-9 ; Rev. xxii. 1-5.

" Lord, to whom shall we go ? Thou hast the words of eternal life."

O Heavenly Father, I thank Thee that in the darkness Thy children can turn to Thee. For the infinite compassion of Thy love made known to us in Jesus Christ, I give Thee thanks. For Jesus kneeling in the shadow of Gethsemane, for Jesus' agony and death upon the Cross, for Jesus risen and alive for evermore, calling us to share His perfect life, I praise and bless Thy Name.

God, my Father, Who knowest all things, I come to Thee now with sorrow in my heart. Thou knowest the confusion and pain of it : the shrinking from the loneliness of the future ; the regrets and the bitter longing. Grant me courage for the days that lie ahead. May I learn to see Thee in the darkness. Help me to be sure that we can never lose any precious gift of Thine and that our loved ones are ours for evermore. For the light and joy and peace of the Father's Home, for the great company of the redeemed who are in Thy presence, and for our own dear one who now sees Thy face, I thank Thee, O Father. For every remembrance of *him*, for every word and act of *his* love, for all the common things of every day we shared, and all the great experiences of joy and sorrow, I thank Thee out of a full heart.

O Father of our Lord and Saviour, Jesus Christ, Whose tender mercy is over all Thy works, and Whose power can turn the shadow of death into morning, to Thy mercy and Thy power I trust myself and all who share my sorrow. In Jesus' Name. Amen.

FOR PRIVATE NOTES

FOR PRIVATE NOTES

FOR PRIVATE NOTES

FOR PRIVATE NOTES